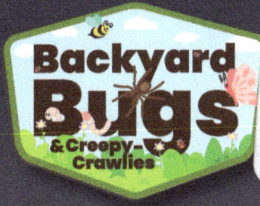

Backyard
Bugs
& Creepy
Crawlies

Ants

Ava Podmorow

Explore other books at:
WWW.ENGAGEBOOKS.COM

VANCOUVER, B.C.

e↗ WWW.ENGAGEBOOKS.COM

Ants: Level Pre-1
Backyard Bugs & Creepy Crawlies
Podmorow, Ava 2004 –
Text © 2022 Engage Books
Design © 2022 Engage Books

Edited by: A.R. Roumanis
and Sarah Harvey

Text set in Epilogue

FIRST EDITION / FIRST PRINTING

LIBRARY AND ARCHIVES CANADA CATALOGUING IN PUBLICATION

Title: Ants / Ava Podmorow.
Names: Podmorow, Ava, author.
Description: Series statement: Backyard bugs & creepy-crawlies
Engaging readers: level pre-1, beginner.

Identifiers: Canadiana (print) 20220403554 | Canadiana (ebook) 20220403562
ISBN 978-1-77476-732-0 (hardcover)
ISBN 978-1-77476-733-7 (softcover)
ISBN 978-1-77476-734-4 (epub)
ISBN 978-1-77476-735-1 (pdf)

Subjects:
LCSH: Ants—Juvenile literature.

Classification: LCC QL568.F7 P63 2022 | DDC J595.79/6—DC23

This project has been made possible in part by the Government of Canada.

Canada

The ants go marching one by one.

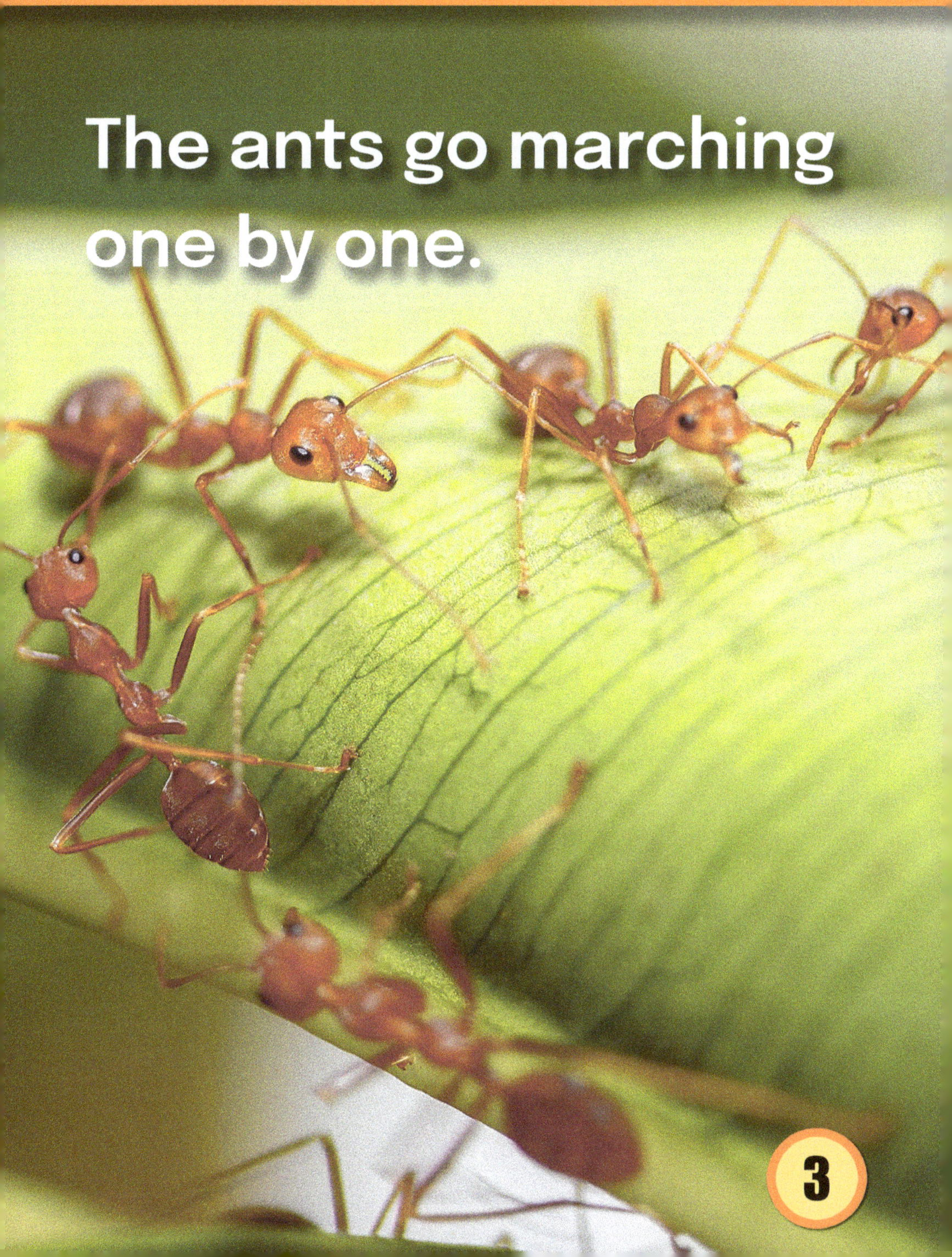

Ants have six legs, two antennae, and two mandibles.

Legs

Stinger

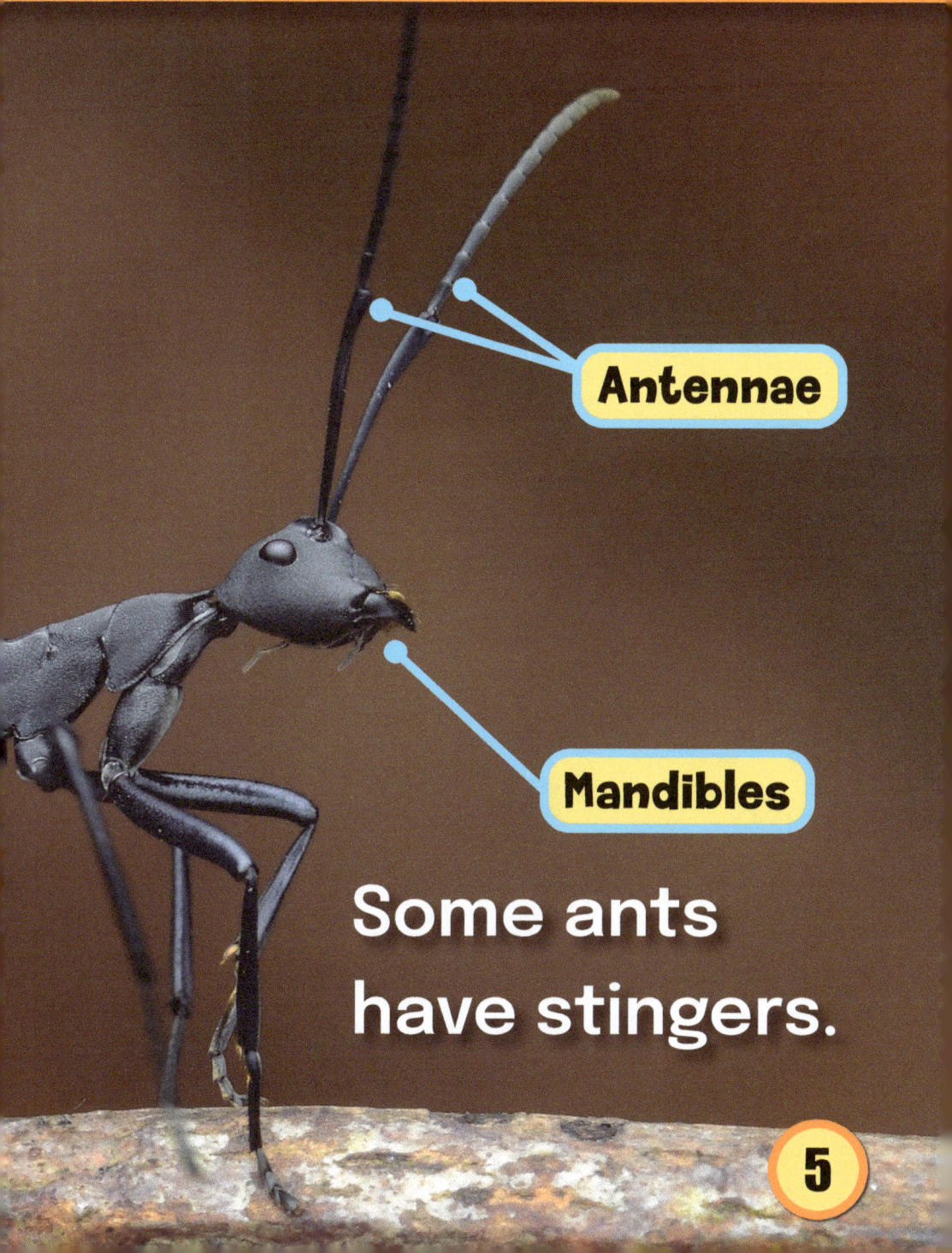

Antennae

Mandibles

Some ants
have stingers.

Ants can be as small as a crumb.

Others can be a bit larger than a bee.

There are over 12,000 kinds of ants in the world.

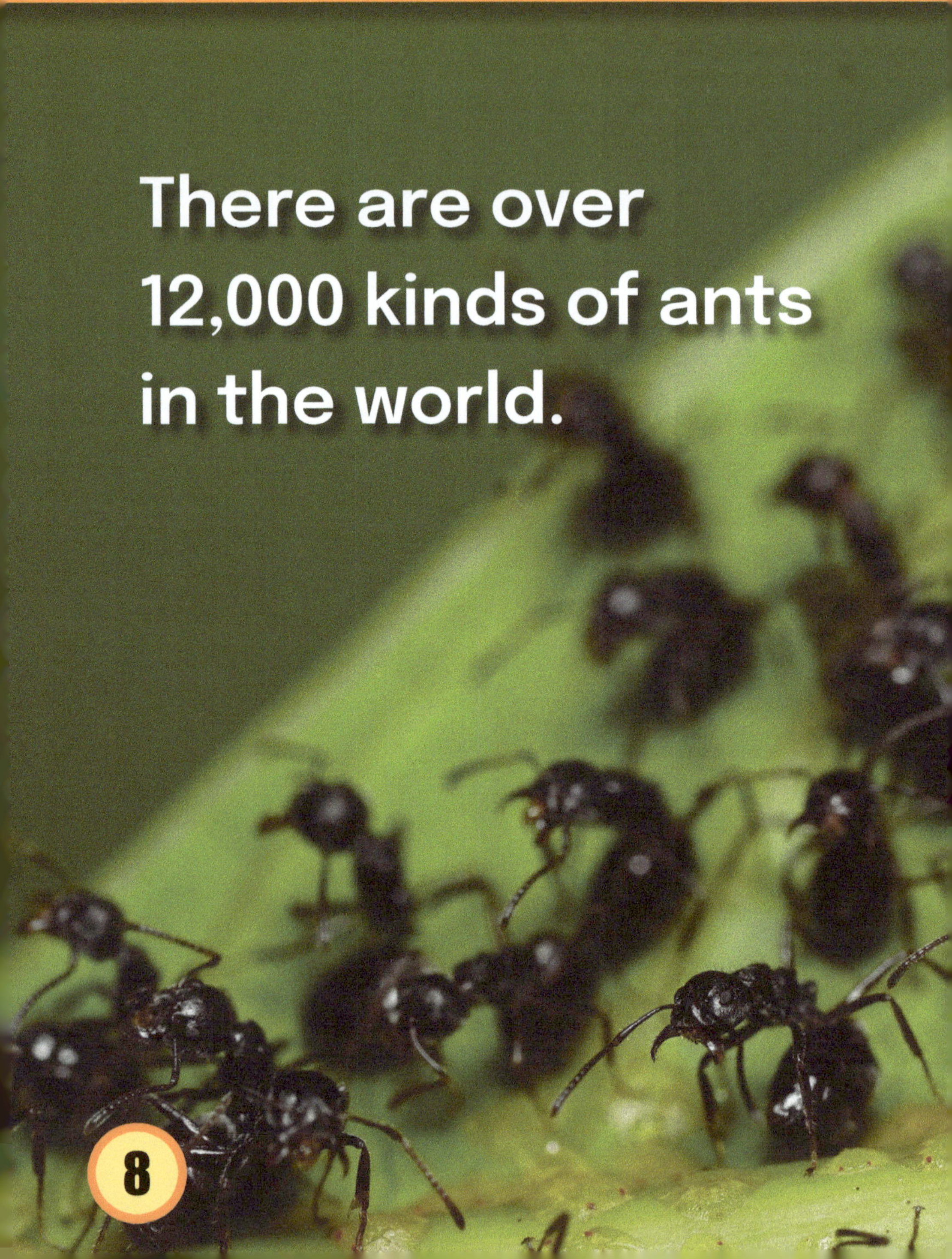

The black garden ant is the most common kind.

Ants like living near houses.

They can always
find food there.

Ants use their sense of smell to find sugary food.

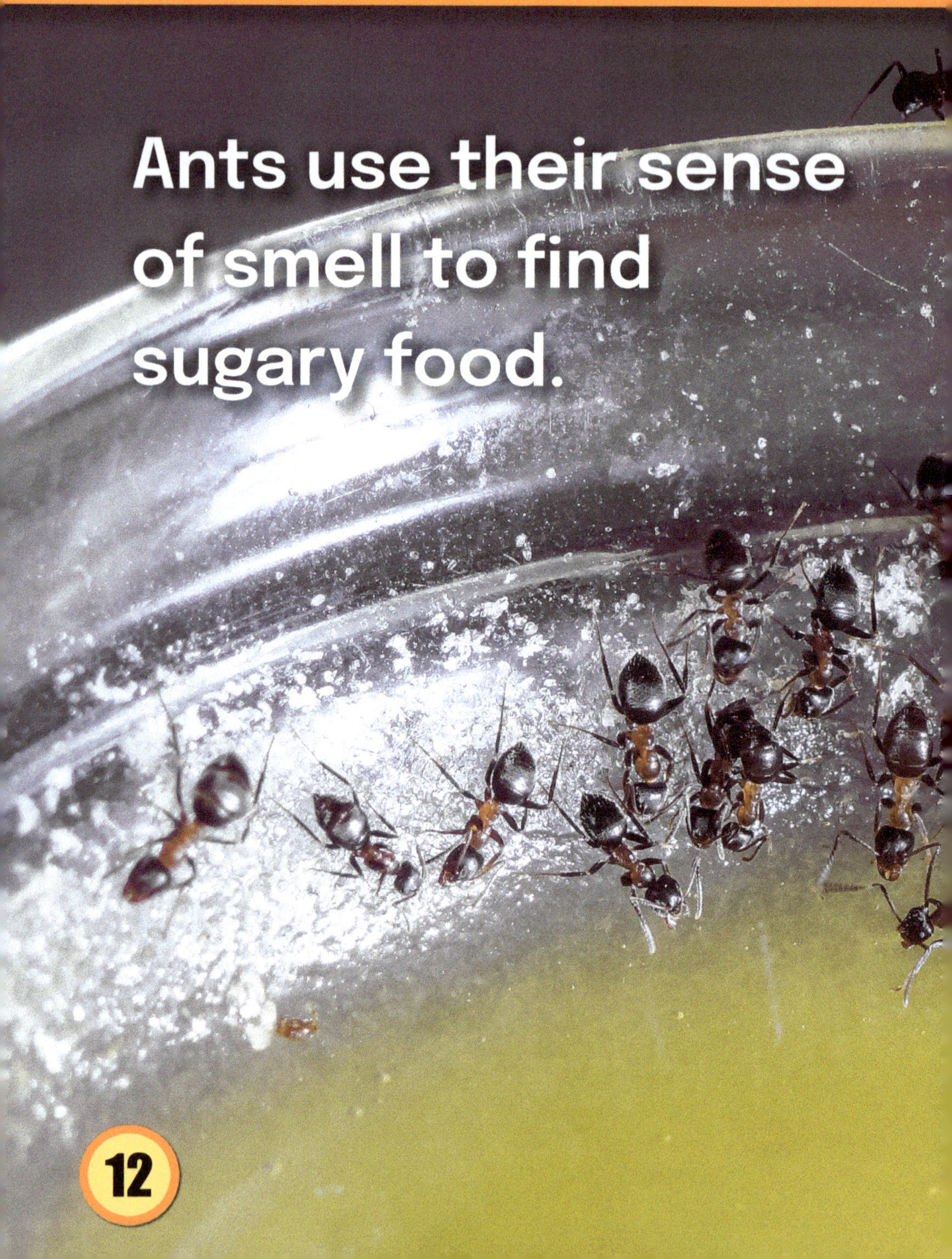

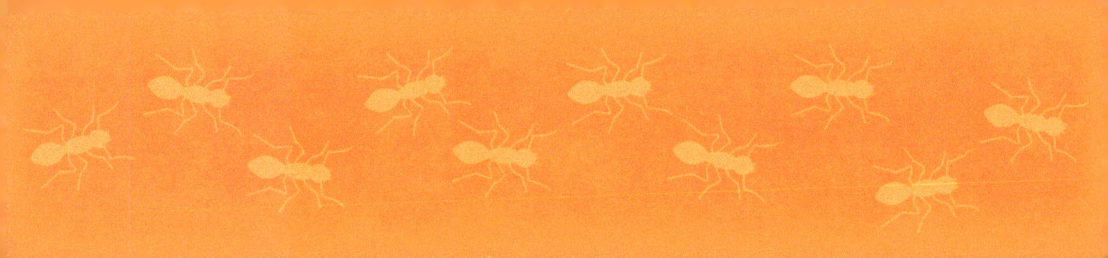

Ants live together in colonies.

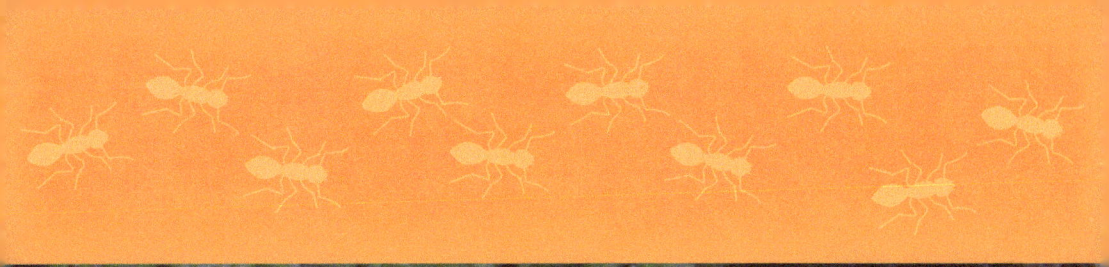

Colony

Some colonies
are huge.

All ants do is work, eat, and sleep.

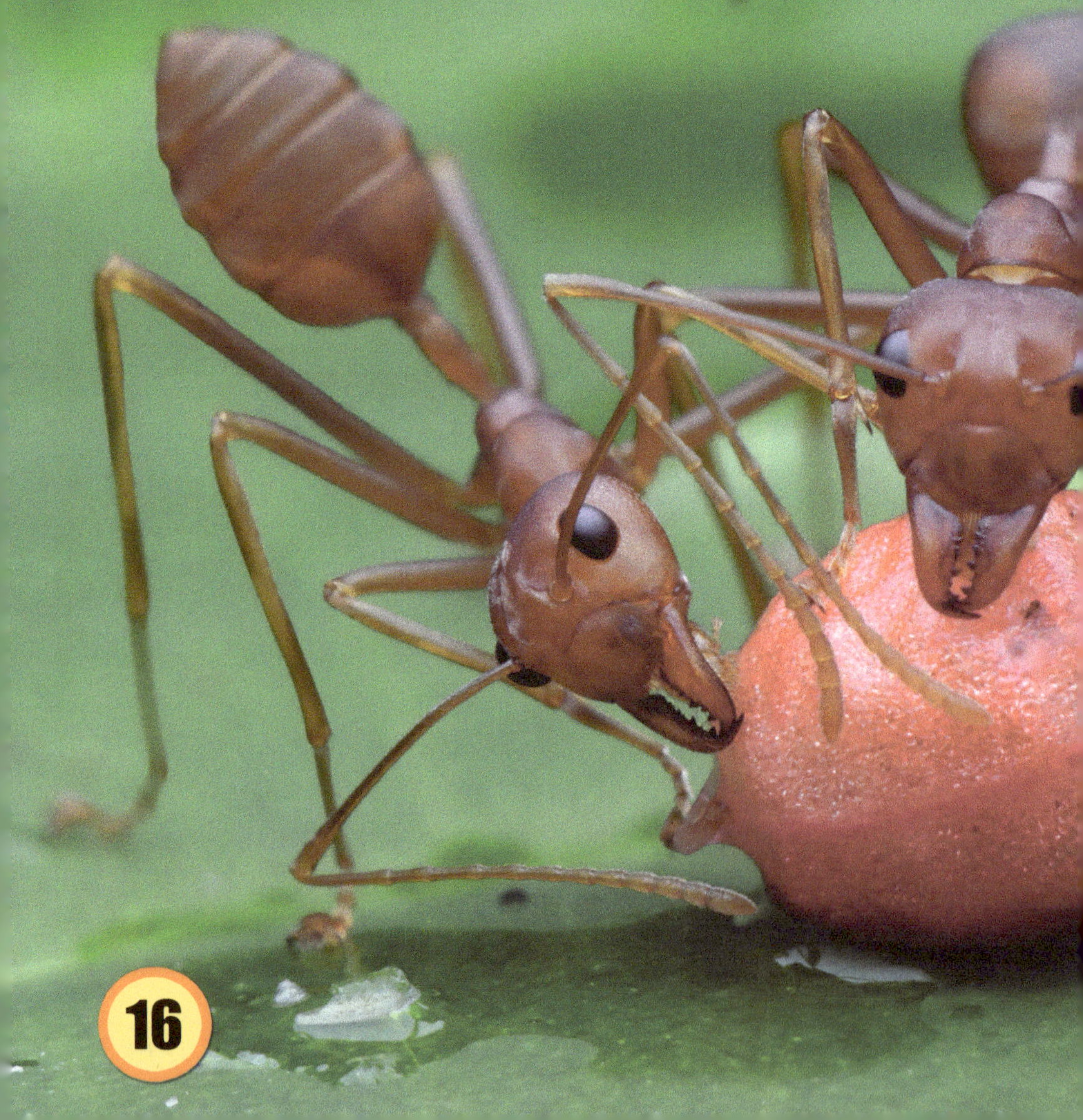

When they wake up they yawn and stretch!

Ants can carry about 50 times their own weight.

Some ants are able to swim.

They can also float
for a long time.

Carpenter ants make tunnels in wood.

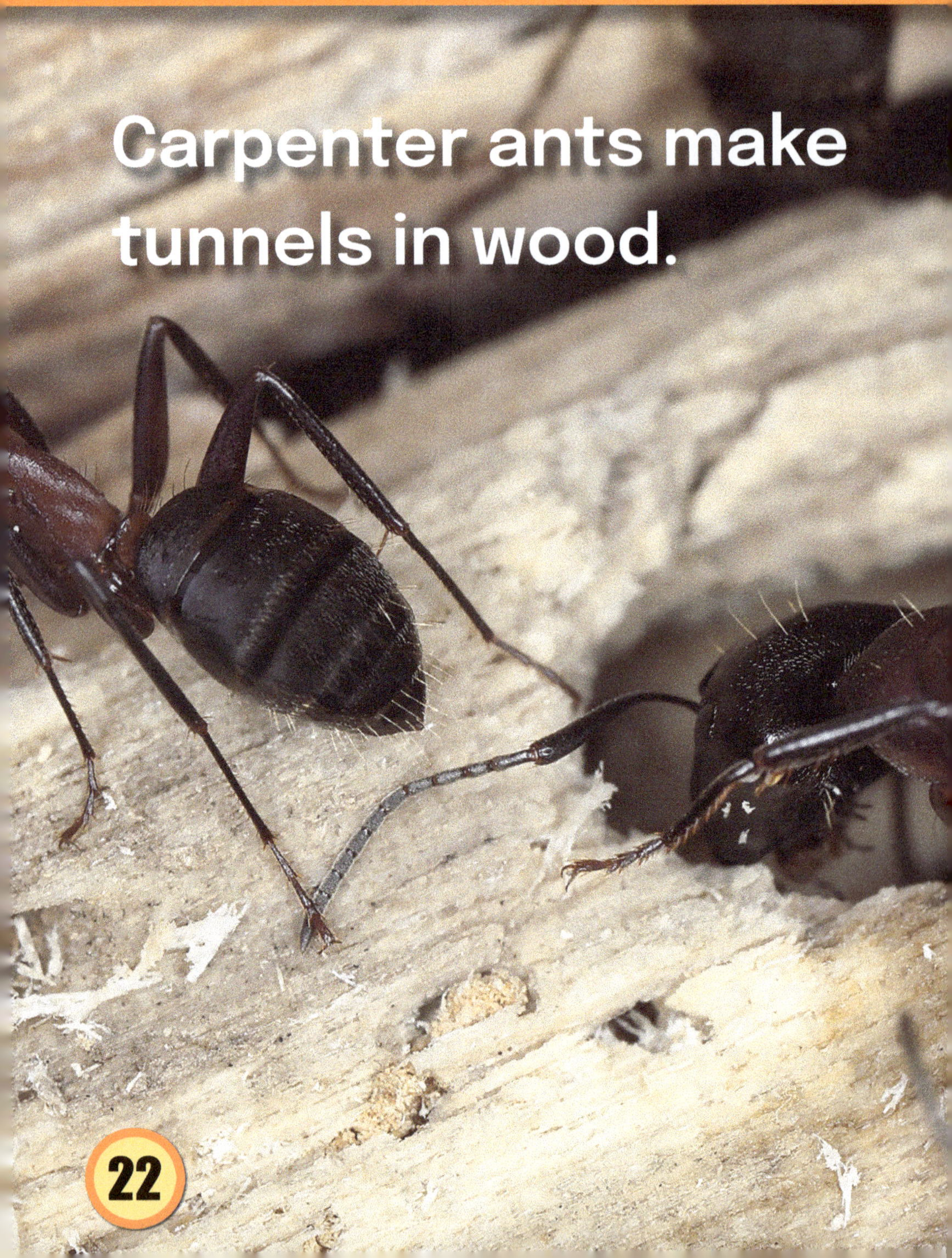

They can do a
lot of damage to
wooden buildings.

23

A group of ants is
called an army.

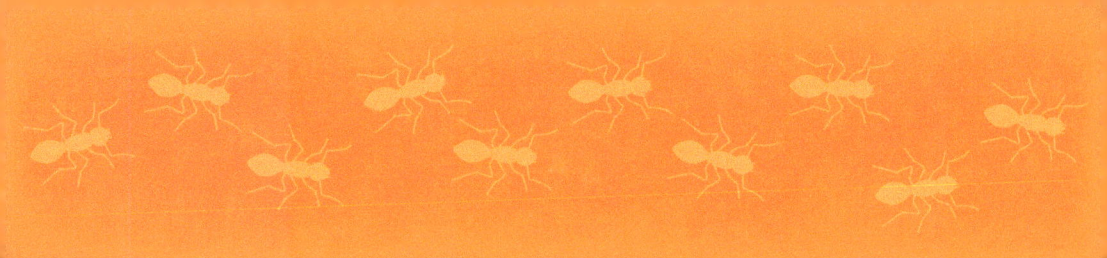

Queen

A female ant is called a queen.

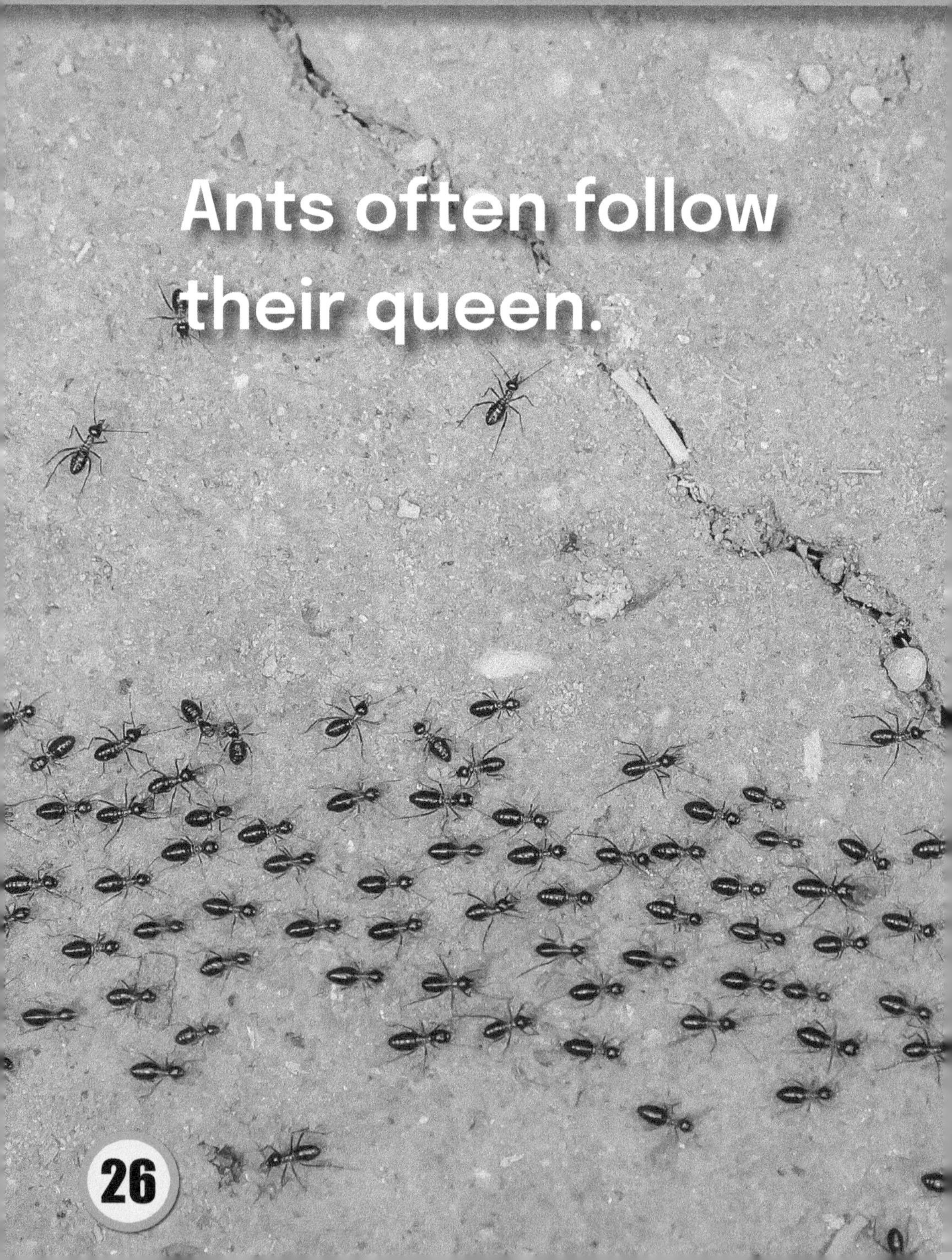

Ants often follow their queen.

She leads them to food.

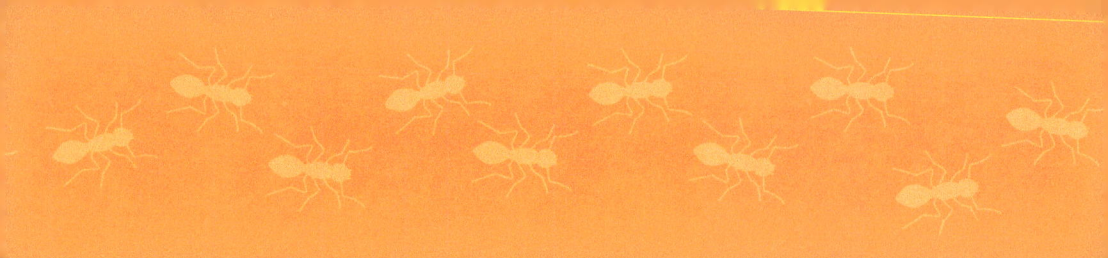

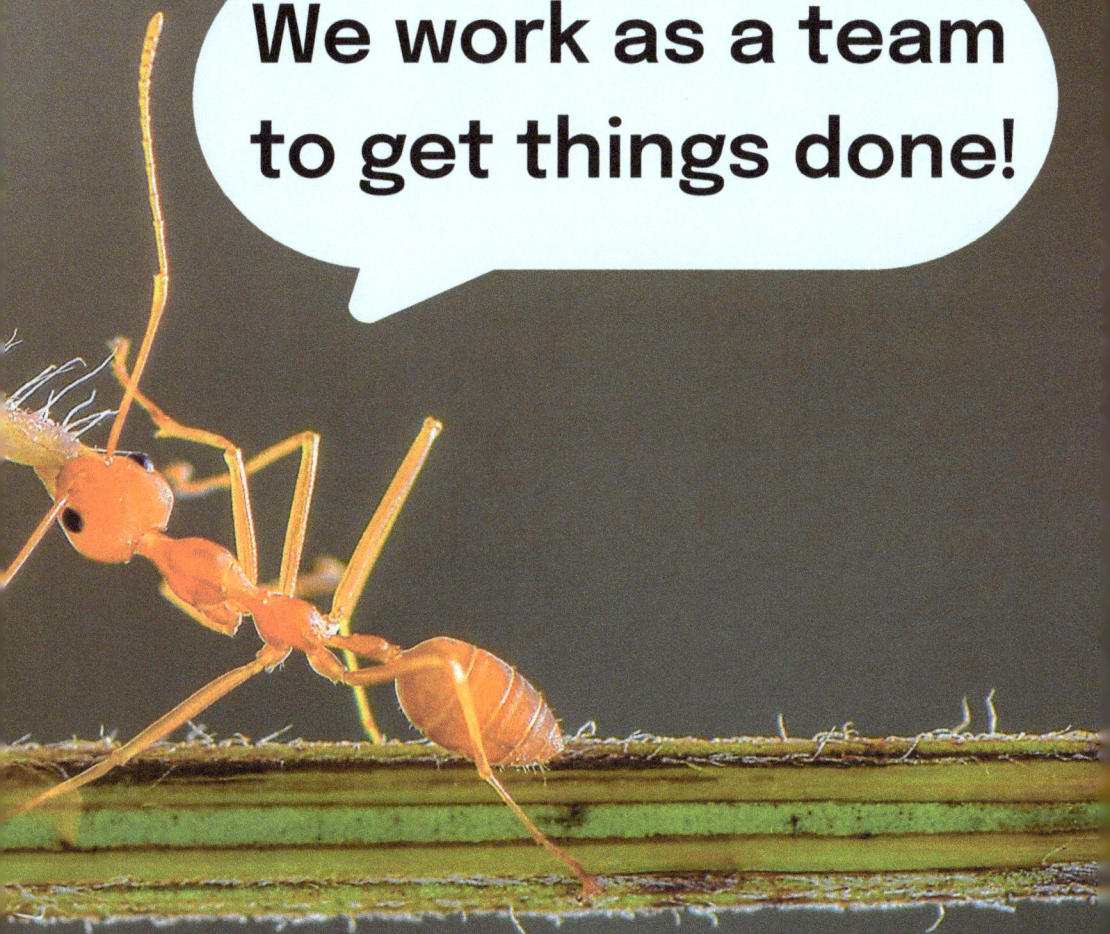

We work as a team to get things done!

Explore other books in the Backyard Bugs & Creepy Crawlies series!

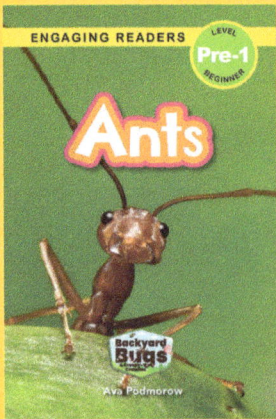

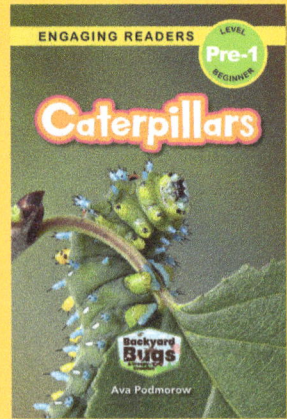

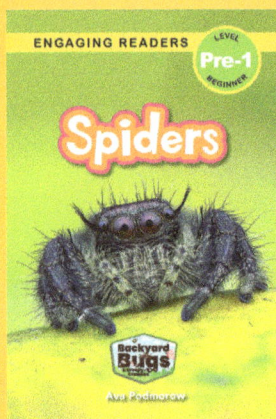

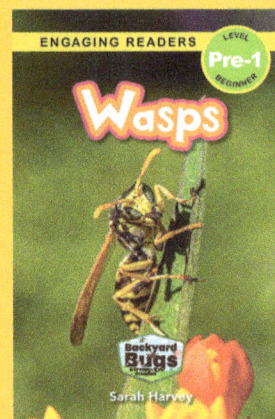

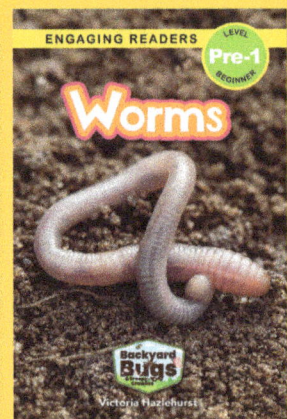

Visit www.engagebooks.com/readers

Explore books in the Animals In The City series.

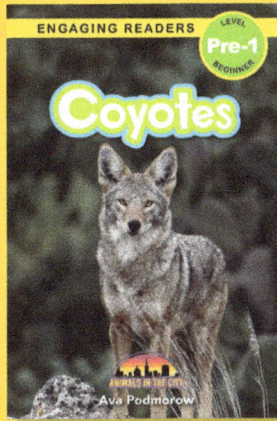

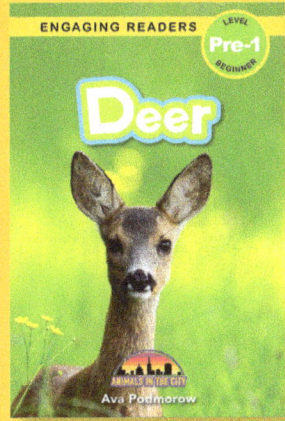

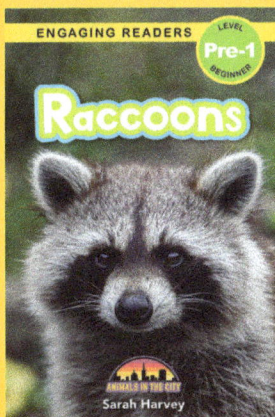

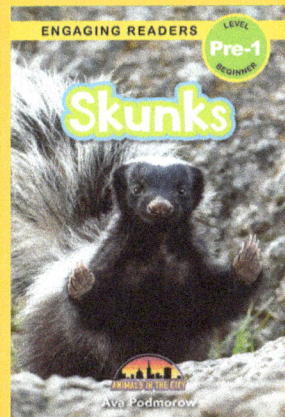

ENGAGING READERS — LEVEL Pre-1 BEGINNER
Cats
Ava Podmorow

ENGAGING READERS — LEVEL Pre-1 BEGINNER
Coyotes
Ava Podmorow

ENGAGING READERS — LEVEL Pre-1 BEGINNER
Deer
Ava Podmorow

ENGAGING READERS — LEVEL Pre-1 BEGINNER
Owls
Ava Podmorow

ENGAGING READERS — LEVEL Pre-1 BEGINNER
Pigeons
Ava Podmorow

ENGAGING READERS — LEVEL Pre-1 BEGINNER
Rabbits
Ava Podmorow

ENGAGING READERS — LEVEL Pre-1 BEGINNER
Raccoons
Sarah Harvey

ENGAGING READERS — LEVEL Pre-1 BEGINNER
Rats
Ava Podmorow

ENGAGING READERS — LEVEL Pre-1 BEGINNER
Skunks
Ava Podmorow

Visit www.engagebooks.com/readers

www.ingramcontent.com/pod-product-compliance
Lightning Source LLC
Chambersburg PA
CBHW040226040426
42331CB00039B/3367